LISA NIESCHLAG ★ LARS WENTRUP

NEW YORK
CHRISTMAS BAKING

PHOTOGRAPHY
LISA NIESCHLAG AND JULIA CAWLEY

RECIPE DEVELOPMENT
AGNES PRUS

murdoch books
Sydney | London

CONTENTS

SWEET CHRISTMAS COOKIES
Whoopie pies, snickerdoodles & co.

HOLIDAY CAKES
Pies, cupcakes & co.

CHRISTMAS BREAKFAST
Breads, muffins & buns

Stories

A SWEET TREAT

New York has put on its finest. The city sparkles and shimmers as Christmas carols echo between one shop and the next. The brightly lit streets are a firework of festive colours. This iconic metropolis attracts people from all over the world.

People come to this pulsating city to experience it first-hand when it is at its most magical, and to marvel at its lavish Christmas decorations, oversized Christmas trees and glittering shopping malls and hotels. New York at Christmas puts on the ultimate show! The city is flooded with lights, and festively lit wreaths and trees decorate its apartment blocks and public spaces, among them Grand Central Station and the world-famous Rockefeller Center.

But the wonder of a New York Christmas is also felt away from the city's bustle.

While New York is the city that never sleeps and may seem to be the antithesis of calm and serenity for most of the year, that all changes when Christmas comes. Suddenly there are moments of peace and harmony popping up, on the chic Upper West Side just as much as in trendy Soho or Brooklyn. The best recipe for finding these magical moments is to allow yourself to be carried along by the city's flow, aimlessly and without pressure of any kind. Our photographer Julia Cawley was only too happy to do so. Having lived in New York for five years, she and her family recently relocated to Hamburg, but she is happy about any excuse to go back to her second home.

We have also come to feel at home in New York. *New York Christmas,* our first New York cookbook, was a culinary portrait of the Big Apple's festive season, from hearty spaghetti and meatballs to spicy pumpkin soup and irresistible cookies and brownies. The book was a great success, and people loved it. That's why we have now created a cookbook of New York's best baking recipes for the Christmas season.

New York Christmas Baking is our surrender to all of the sweet temptations that the city – and the USA – has to offer. At the same time, this book has invited us to revisit delightful memories from our childhoods: as Lisa styled and photographed these delicacies, she reminisced about the smell of the Christmas cookies her grandmother, a true New Yorker, used to bake. Her thoughts drifted back, across the ocean, to the beloved smells of that Manhattan apartment, to family traditions of the sweetest and fondest kind.

Sweet dreams, fresh from New York: join us on another journey to this amazing city, which invites people to dream and indulge like no other.

Sweet Christmas!

Lisa Nieschlag and Lars Wentrup

LARS WENTRUP

LISA NIESCHLAG

JULIA CAWLEY

Happy Holidays!

A Christmas Memory

Truman Capote

knew it before I got out of bed," she says, turning away from the window with a purposeful excitement in her eyes. "The courthouse bell sounded so cold and clear. And there were no birds singing; they've gone to warmer country, yes indeed. Oh, Buddy, stop stuffing biscuits and fetch our buggy. Help me find my hat. We've thirty cakes to bake."

It's always the same: a morning arrives in November, and my friend, as though officially inaugurating the Christmas time of year that exhilarates her imagination and fuels the blaze of her heart, announces: "It's fruit-cake weather! Fetch our buggy. Help me find my hat."

The hat is found, a straw cartwheel corsaged with velvet roses out-of-doors has faded: it once belonged to a more fashionable relative. Together, we guide our buggy, a dilapidated baby carriage, out to the garden and into a grove of pecan trees. The buggy is mine; that is, it was bought for me when I was born. It is made of wicker, rather unravelled, and the wheels wobble like a drunkard's legs. But it is a faithful object; springtimes, we take it to the woods and fill it with flowers, herbs, wild fern for our porch pots; in the summer, we pile it with picnic paraphernalia and sugar-cane fishing poles and roll it down to the edge of a creek; it has its winter uses, too: as a truck for hauling firewood from the yard to the kitchen, as a warm bed for Queenie, our tough little orange and white rat terrier who has survived distemper and two rattlesnake bites. Queenie is trotting beside it now.

Three hours later we are back in the kitchen hulling a heaping buggyload of windfall pecans. Our backs hurt from gathering them: how hard they were to find (the main crop having been shaken off the trees and sold by the orchard's owners, who are not us)

among the concealing leaves, the frosted, deceiving grass. Caarackle! A cheery crunch, scraps of miniature thunder sound as the shells collapse and the golden mound of sweet oily ivory meat mounts in the milk-glass bowl. Queenie begs to taste, and now and again my friend sneaks her a mite, though insisting we deprive ourselves. "We mustn't, Buddy. If we start, we won't stop. And there's scarcely enough as there is. For thirty cakes." The kitchen is growing dark. Dusk turns the window into a mirror: our reflections mingle with the rising moon as we work by the fire-side in the firelight. At last, when the moon is quite high, we toss the final hull into the fire and, with joined sighs, watch it catch flame. The buggy is empty, the bowl is brimful.

We eat our supper (cold biscuits, bacon, blackberry jam) and discuss tomorrow. Tomorrow the kind of work I like best begins: buying. Cherries and citron, ginger and vanilla and canned Hawaiian pineapple, rinds and raisins and walnuts and whiskey and oh, so much flour, butter, so many eggs, spices, flavourings: why, we'll need a pony to pull the buggy home. ★

SWEET CHRISTMAS COOKIES

WHOOPIE PIES, SNICKERDOODLES & CO.

CANDY CANE COOKIES

No New York Christmas tree would be complete without red and white striped candy canes. Inspired by the ubiquitous Christmas sweets, these candy cane cookies are not only a true eye-catcher on any cookie platter, they can also be hung on your mug of tea or coffee or served with a hot chocolate with marshmallow topping.

Add the butter and icing sugar to a bowl. Beat until creamy, about 3 minutes, then add the egg, vanilla and almond extract and beat for 1 minute.

Sift the flour, baking powder and salt together in another bowl until combined. Mix, a little at a time, into the butter-sugar-egg mixture.

Transfer half of the dough to a separate bowl. Add the red colouring and mix well. Wrap each piece of dough in plastic wrap and refrigerate for about 4 hours.

Preheat the oven to 175°C (345°F) and line two baking trays with baking paper. With your hands, shape the dough into several thin strands, about 12 cm (4½ inches) long and 5 mm (¼ inch) thick. Twist one plain and one red strand around each other to make each cookie, curving to make a candy cane shape. Place on a baking tray and sprinkle with sugar. Bake the cookies in the oven for about 10 minutes.

INGREDIENTS

Makes about 45

225 g (8 oz) butter, at
room temperature
170 g icing (confectioners')
sugar
1 egg
2 tsp vanilla extract
A few drops of almond extract
(or natural almond flavour)
470 g (15 oz) plain flour
2 tsp baking powder
¼ tsp salt
½ tsp red food colouring (or
2 tsp beetroot powder)

Also:
Raw sugar for sprinkling

LEMON COOKIES

Lemon cookies make for a refreshing change from the usual rich Christmas sweets. Lemon juice and zest give them a delicate citrus aroma, and these cookies are very quick and easy to make. Our tip: the flavoured sugar is perfect for sweetening tea or iced tea, so it's a good idea to make more than you need for the recipe. Simply transfer the grated zest of one lemon and some sugar to a jar and seal well for storage. Shake the jar occasionally to distribute the flavour evenly.

INGREDIENTS

Makes about 45

120 g (4¼ oz) raw sugar
Grated zest of 1–2 lemons
220 g (7¾ oz) plain flour
¼ tsp baking powder
¼ tsp salt
150 g (5½ oz) cold butter,
finely diced
2 Tbsp lemon juice
1 egg yolk
½ tsp vanilla extract

For the icing:
150 g (5½ oz) icing
(confectioners') sugar
2 Tbsp lemon juice
1 Tbsp cream cheese

Put the sugar and lemon zest into a food processor and pulse for about 30 seconds until the lemon zest is evenly distributed throughout the sugar. Alternatively, mix the sugar and lemon zest in a mortar and pestle or a small bowl.

Combine the flour, baking powder and salt in a bowl. Stir in the lemon-flavoured sugar. Add the butter and use your fingers or a fork to combine everything quickly to a crumble. Stir in the lemon juice, egg yolk and vanilla extract. Shape the dough into a roll about 4 cm (1½ inches) thick. Wrap in foil and freeze for 1 hour.

Preheat the oven to 180°C (350°F) and line two baking trays with baking paper. Cut the frozen dough into slices about 5 mm (¼ inch) thick. Transfer the slices onto the trays, setting them a little apart, and bake for 10–12 minutes. Remove from the oven and leave to cool completely.

For the icing, place the icing sugar in a bowl. Add the lemon juice and cream cheese and stir well to combine. Drizzle the icing over the cookies. Leave to dry for at least 1 hour.

SUGAR COOKIES

Everybody loves sugar cookies, young and old, and Christmas wouldn't be quite the same without them. They are a must for any Christmas cookie platter, along with cookie cups and whoopie pies. The dough is very easy to make, and you can be as creative as you like with the cookie decorations.

Combine the flour with the baking powder, bicarbonate of soda and salt in a mixing bowl and set aside. Beat the butter and sugar until creamy, about 3 minutes. Add the egg and beat for 1 minute to combine. Stir in the vanilla extract and lemon zest, then add the flour mixture and cream alternately in two batches. Wrap the dough in plastic wrap and rest it in the refrigerator for at least 2 hours, preferably overnight.

Preheat the oven to 180°C (350°F) and line two baking trays with baking paper. Roll out the dough about 3 mm (⅛ inch) thick on a lightly floured surface and use a cookie cutter to cut out stars, circles or other shapes. Transfer the cookies onto the trays and dust with a little icing sugar. Moisten a pastry brush with a little water. Brush the cookies and dust again with some more icing sugar. Bake in the preheated oven until golden brown, about 10 minutes. Remove from the oven and dust with more icing sugar to taste.

Tip: Use plain or coloured icing instead of icing sugar to decorate the cookies after baking.

INGREDIENTS

Makes about 30

270 g (9½ oz) plain flour
½ tsp baking powder
¼ tsp bicarbonate of soda
(baking soda)
¼ tsp salt
120 g (4¼ oz) butter, at room
temperature
150 g (5½ oz) raw sugar
1 egg
1 tsp vanilla extract
1 tsp grated lemon zest,
to taste
60 ml (2 fl oz) single (pure)
cream

Also:
Flour for dusting
Icing (confectioners') sugar

SOUR CREAM SNOWFLAKES

While we were working on this book, Julia was desperate for some snow to be able to photograph the Big Apple in its full, white glory. No doubt she would have loved to sweeten the wait with these pretty cookies. From our own experience, we can confidently say that these snowflakes, lovingly decorated with icing and shimmery sprinkles, are very popular.

INGREDIENTS

Makes about 40

120 g (4¼ oz) butter, at
room temperature
160 g (5½ oz) raw sugar
1 egg yolk
½ tsp vanilla extract
240 g (8½ oz) sour cream,
at room temperature
400 g (14 oz) plain flour
½ tsp baking powder
¼ tsp bicarbonate of soda
(baking soda)
1 pinch freshly grated
nutmeg

For the icing:
120 g (4¼ oz) icing
(confectioners') sugar
1 Tbsp butter, melted
¼ tsp vanilla extract
About 1 Tbsp milk

Also:
Flour for dusting
Silver sprinkles

Beat the butter and sugar in a bowl until creamy, about 3 minutes. Stir in the egg yolk and vanilla extract followed by the sour cream, and combine well. Combine the flour with the baking powder, bicarbonate of soda, nutmeg and a pinch of salt and briefly stir the mixture into the wet ingredients. Wrap the dough in plastic wrap and rest it in the refrigerator overnight.

Preheat the oven to 175°C (345°F) and line a baking tray with baking paper. Sprinkle the work surface and a rolling pin with flour. Roll out the dough about 5 mm (¼ inch) thick and use a cookie cutter to cut out snowflake shapes. It's normal for the dough to stick. Transfer the cookies onto the tray and bake for about 10 minutes. Don't let them brown too much. Remove from the oven and leave to cool fully on a wire rack.

For the icing, sift the icing sugar into a bowl. Add the butter and vanilla extract and whisk until smooth. Stir in a little milk until the icing has the desired consistency. Decorate the cookies with the icing and silver sprinkles. Store in a tin between sheets of baking paper, in a cool place.

STAINED-GLASS COOKIES

If you're looking to make some special Christmas cookies, try these pretty stained-glass cookies. The powdered lollies melt in the oven to create colourful little 'windows'. They also make lovely Christmas tree decorations: simply make a hole in the cookies before baking and then pull some pretty ribbon through the hole.

Combine the flour with the baking powder and salt in a mixing bowl and set aside. Beat the butter and sugar in a separate bowl until creamy, about 3 minutes. Beat in the egg, vanilla extract and lemon zest. Fold in the flour mixture in two batches to make a smooth dough. Wrap in plastic wrap and rest in the refrigerator for 2 hours.

Preheat the oven to 160°C (320°F) and line two baking trays with baking paper. Sort the lollies by colour and pulse to a fine powder in a small food processor. Transfer to bowls, separated by colour. Dust your benchtop lightly with flour, roll the dough out thinly, about 3 mm (1/8 inch), and use a cookie cutter to cut out shapes, such as Christmas trees, stars or baubles.

Transfer the cookies onto the trays. Cut out small shapes from inside the cookies and fill these with a little of the powdered lollies. If you are planning to use the cookies as decorations, also make a small hole for the ribbon. Bake until golden brown, about 10 minutes, and leave to cool on the trays.

INGREDIENTS

Makes about 60

300 g (10½ oz) plain flour
¼ tsp baking powder
¼ tsp salt
200 g (7 oz) butter, at
room temperature
120 g (4¼ oz) raw sugar
1 egg
1½ tsp vanilla extract
¼ tsp grated lemon zest
About 180 g (6 oz) hard lollies
in various colours

Also:
Flour for dusting

COCONUT MACAROONS

Making the batter for these coconut macaroons over a pan of boiling water keeps them deliciously moist on the inside. They crisp up beautifully on the outside during baking and are best eaten on the day of baking. Use a soft touch when shaping the dough: always moisten your hands with a little water and use gentle pressure to flatten the balls into macaroon shapes.

INGREDIENTS

Makes about 20

120 g (4¼ oz) desiccated coconut
60 g (2¼ oz) coconut chips (or flaked or desiccated coconut)
120 g (4¼ oz) raw sugar
3 egg whites
1 tsp vanilla extract
¼ tsp salt

Also:
About 150 g (5½ oz) dark chocolate, finely chopped

Put the desiccated coconut, coconut chips, sugar, egg whites, vanilla extract and salt in a heatproof bowl and mix thoroughly. Set the bowl over a saucepan of simmering water and cook, stirring constantly, for about 10 minutes or until the mixture feels hot. Remove from the heat, cover and set aside to rest at room temperature for 30 minutes.

Preheat the oven to 180°C (350°F) and line a baking tray with baking paper. Use a teaspoon or moistened fingers to remove small quantities of the coconut batter. Roll into balls and place the macaroons on the tray using gentle pressure. Keep cleaning and moistening your hands as you go. Bake the macaroons for about 7 minutes, then reduce the temperature to 160°C (320°F) and bake for another 5 minutes or until they start taking on a little colour. Remove from the oven and leave the macaroons to cool on a wire rack.

Melt 100 g (3½ oz) of the chocolate, then add the remaining chocolate, stirring until all the chocolate has melted. Dip the macaroons into the chocolate and leave to set on a tray lined with baking paper.

PUMPKIN SPICE WHOOPIE PIES

In the US, pumpkin purée is a popular ingredient for pies and cakes and is readily available in tins. You may be able to find it in a supermarket, but it is easy enough to make yourself. We recommend that you make a larger quantity because pumpkin purée freezes very well.

Prepare the pumpkin purée and filling one day ahead. Preheat the oven to 180°C (350°F) and line a baking tray with baking paper. Cut the pumpkin in half and discard the seeds. Place on the tray, cut side down, and roast until soft, about 40 minutes. Scrape out the pumpkin flesh with a spoon and mash finely. Measure out 180 g (6 oz) of the pumpkin purée and refrigerate overnight. Freeze the remainder or use it for another recipe (e.g. Cinnamon roll pancakes, page 111).

To make the filling, heat the butter in a small saucepan until it browns. Remove from the heat and set aside to cool. Beat in the cream cheese, maple syrup and cinnamon until creamy, about 2 minutes. Gradually stir in the icing sugar. Cover and refrigerate overnight.

Preheat the oven to 180°C (350°F) and line two baking trays with baking paper. Combine the flour, baking powder, bicarbonate of soda, salt and spices in a bowl and set aside. Whisk the two types of sugar with the oil for 1 minute, then stir in the eggs, one at a time, whisking about 30 seconds each. Add the pumpkin purée, vanilla extract, orange zest and ginger. Fold in the flour mixture in two batches.

Use a small ice cream scoop or a teaspoon to divide the dough into 30 portions. Shape these into balls with moistened hands and transfer to the baking tray. Flatten gently and bake for about 11 minutes. Remove from the oven and leave to cool completely.

Spread the filling over half of the cookies, then top with the remaining cookies.

INGREDIENTS

Makes 15

800 g (1 lb 12 oz) pumpkin
200 g (7 oz) plain flour
½ tsp baking powder
½ tsp bicarbonate of soda
(baking soda)
½ tsp salt
2 tsp ground cinnamon
½ tsp ground allspice
¼ tsp ground cloves
¼ tsp freshly grated nutmeg
100 g (3½ oz) dark brown sugar
50 g (1¾ oz) sugar
120 ml (4 fl oz) oil
2 eggs
1 tsp vanilla extract
Grated zest of ½ orange
½ tsp grated fresh ginger

For the filling:
40 g (1½ oz) butter
60 g (2¼ oz) cream cheese
1 Tbsp maple syrup
½ tsp ground cinnamon
25 g (1 oz) icing
(confectioners') sugar

SNOWBALL COOKIES

Let it snow! These small snowball-shaped cookies are rolled in icing sugar spiced with cardamom and cinnamon after baking. You can substitute the almonds in the recipe with pecans, walnuts or hazelnuts and use orange zest instead of the lemon zest, if preferred.

INGREDIENTS

Makes about 30

3 Tbsp chopped almonds
90 g (3¼ oz) plain flour
65 g (2¼ oz) ground almonds
½ tsp ground cardamom
½ tsp ground cinnamon
½ tsp ground allspice
¼ tsp ground ginger
¼ tsp freshly grated nutmeg
¼ tsp salt
110 g (3¾ oz) butter,
at room temperature
25 g (1 oz) icing
(confectioners') sugar
½ tsp vanilla extract
Grated zest of ½ lemon

Also:
About 100 g (3½ oz) icing
(confectioners') sugar
¼ tsp ground cardamom
¼ tsp ground cinnamon

Dry-roast the chopped almonds in a frying pan over medium heat until golden brown. Remove from the heat and set aside to cool.

Thoroughly combine the flour with the ground and chopped almonds, spices and salt in a mixing bowl. Beat the butter in a separate bowl until creamy, about 2 minutes. Gradually stir in first the icing sugar, then the vanilla extract and lemon zest. Fold in the almond and flour mixture, cover and leave to rest in the refrigerator for 30 minutes.

Preheat the oven to 160°C (320°F) and line a baking tray with baking paper. Combine the extra icing sugar with the cardamom and cinnamon, sift into a shallow bowl and set aside. Remove the dough from the refrigerator and use a teaspoon to divide it into small portions. Use moistened hands to shape these into walnut-sized balls. Transfer the cookie balls onto the tray and bake until golden brown, about 18 minutes. Remove from the oven and leave to cool for 2 minutes.

Toss the warm cookie balls in the spiced icing sugar. Leave to cool for another 15 minutes on a wire rack and then toss again in the icing sugar mixture. These cookies taste best if left to develop their flavour overnight.

BISCOTTI WITH PISTACHIOS & CRANBERRIES

Biscotti are a delicious version of the famous Italian cantuccini biscuits. Green pistachios and red cranberries make this version a perfect Christmas sweet. The crunchy biscuits are also delicious dunked in coffee or espresso. If you don't like cranberries, use other types of dried fruit – there's no limit to your creativity here.

Preheat the oven to 180°C (350°F) and line two baking trays with baking paper. Combine the flour, polenta, baking powder and salt in a mixing bowl and set aside. Beat the butter and sugar in another bowl until light and creamy, about 3 minutes. Stir in the eggs, one at a time, until well combined, then add the orange zest and vanilla extract. Gradually fold in the flour mixture, followed by the pistachios and cranberries. You should end up with a sticky dough. Cover and leave to rest in the refrigerator for 30 minutes.

Halve the dough and form each portion into a small loaf. Moisten your hands a little and smooth out the loaves. Place on the baking trays and bake for 25–30 minutes, until golden brown. Remove from the oven and leave to cool for 15 minutes. Reduce the oven to 160°C (320°F).

Use a serrated knife to cut the loaves into 1.5 cm (½ inch) slices. Return the slices to the trays and bake for 7 minutes, then turn and bake for another 7 minutes. Remove from the oven and leave to cool completely.

Melt half of the white chocolate in a heatproof bowl over a pan of simmering water. Remove the bowl from the pan, add the rest of the chocolate and stir until melted. Dip the base of the biscotti in the melted chocolate and set aside to dry on a wire rack.

INGREDIENTS

Makes about 24

150 g (5½ oz) plain flour
150 g (5½ oz) fine polenta
½ tsp baking powder
½ tsp salt
80 g (2¾ oz) butter, at
room temperature
225 g (8 oz) raw sugar
2 eggs
Grated zest of 1 orange
1 tsp vanilla extract
100 g (3½ oz) pistachio nuts
100 g (3½ oz) dried cranberries

Also:
About 150 g (5½ oz) white
chocolate, finely chopped

BLACK & WHITE COOKIES

These cookies are a true New York classic and sold in just about every bakery. They are not crunchy like other cookies, but soft, moist and cake-like. Once the icing has set, either serve them immediately or store them in an airtight container to prevent them from drying out.

INGREDIENTS

Makes about 24

125 g (4½ oz) plain flour
25 g (1 oz) cornflour
½ tsp bicarbonate of soda
(baking soda)
½ tsp salt
½ tsp vanilla extract
80 ml (2½ fl oz) buttermilk
75 g (2½ oz) butter, at
room temperature
80 g (2¾ oz) raw sugar
1 egg

For the icing:
160 g (5½ oz) + 2 tsp icing
(confectioners') sugar
About 100 ml (3½ fl oz)
boiling water
40 g (1½ oz) dark chocolate,
coarsely chopped
½ tsp maple syrup
1 Tbsp cocoa powder

Preheat the oven to 180°C (350°F) and line two baking trays with baking paper. Combine the flour with the cornflour, bicarbonate of soda and salt in a bowl and set aside. Stir the vanilla extract into the buttermilk in another bowl and set aside.

Beat the butter and sugar until creamy, about 3 minutes, then add the egg and continue to beat for 1 minute. Fold in the flour mixture and buttermilk mixture alternately, in three batches. Transfer the batter to a piping bag and pipe about 24 round heaps onto the trays, spacing them a little apart. Bake on the middle rack, one tray at a time, for about 12 minutes. Leave to cool.

For the icing, sift the 160 g of icing sugar into a bowl. Gradually stir in about 50 ml (1½ fl oz) of the boiling water until you have a thick, spreadable mixture. Turn the cookies upside down and brush half of each with the white icing.

Melt the chocolate in the remaining boiling water. Stir in the maple syrup, cocoa and 2 tsp icing sugar. Leave to cool a little, then use to ice the other half of the cookie bases.

PEANUT BUTTER SANDWICH COOKIES

A creamy peanut butter filling between two chocolate cookies: we love it! In the US, peanut butter is a popular baking ingredient, and we would be very much remiss if we did not include a peanut butter recipe here. You can use either smooth or crunchy peanut butter in this recipe.

Preheat the oven to 180°C (350°F) and line two baking trays with baking paper. Beat the butter and sugars in a bowl until creamy, about 3 minutes. Add the egg and vanilla extract and beat for 1 minute to combine. Sift the flour, cocoa, salt and bicarbonate of soda in another bowl, then fold into the wet ingredients with a wooden spoon.

Shape the dough into walnut-sized balls. Transfer the balls onto the baking trays, flatten gently and bake for about 9 minutes.

Remove the cookies from the oven and leave to cool completely on a wire rack.

For the filling, beat the butter until creamy, about 3 minutes. Stir in the remaining ingredients. Cover the flat bases of half the cookies with the filling, top with the remaining cookies and gently press together.

INGREDIENTS

Makes about 12 double-decker cookies

125 g (4½ oz) butter, at room temperature
80 g (2¾ oz) raw sugar
50 g (1¾ oz) dark brown sugar
1 egg
1 tsp vanilla extract
100 g (3½ oz) plain flour
45 g (1½ oz) cocoa powder
½ tsp salt
¼ tsp bicarbonate of soda (baking soda)

For the filling:
40 g (1½ oz) butter, at room temperature
150 g (5½ oz) peanut butter
50 g (1¾ oz) icing (confectioners') sugar
1 Tbsp milk
½ tsp vanilla extract

GINGER SNAPS WITH WHITE CHOCOLATE

Ginger has been renowned for its health benefits for centuries, and fresh ginger is used in a vast range of dishes from different cuisines. These ginger snaps are made with a triple hit of ground, freshly grated and crystallised ginger to create an amazingly rich flavour.

INGREDIENTS

Makes about 35

300 g (10½ oz) plain flour
2 tsp bicarbonate of soda
(baking soda)
1½ tsp ground ginger
1 tsp ground cinnamon
½ tsp ground cloves
¼ tsp salt
180 g (6 oz) butter, at
room temperature
120 g (4¼ oz) dark brown sugar
1 egg
80 g (2¾ oz) molasses
1½ tsp grated fresh ginger
50 g (1¾ oz) crystallised ginger,
very finely chopped
About 3 Tbsp raw sugar

Also:
About 200 g (7 oz) white
chocolate, finely chopped
About 20 g (¾ oz) crystallised
ginger, very finely chopped

Combine the flour, bicarbonate of soda, ground spices and salt in a bowl and set aside. Beat the butter and brown sugar in a separate bowl until creamy, about 3 minutes. Add the egg and beat for 1 minute to combine. Stir in the molasses and the fresh and crystallised ginger. Fold in the flour mixture in two batches. Cover and leave to rest in the refrigerator for 30 minutes.

Preheat the oven to 180°C (350°F) and line two baking trays with baking paper. Put the raw sugar in a small bowl and set aside.

Use a teaspoon to divide the dough into small portions. Shape these into balls between your hands. Press gently to flatten, then roll in the sugar and transfer to the baking trays, spacing them slightly apart. Bake the cookies for 12–15 minutes. Remove from the oven and leave to cool completely on a wire rack.

Melt about half of the chocolate in a heatproof bowl over a pan of simmering water. Add the remaining chocolate and stir until melted. Dip the ginger snaps into the melted chocolate. Transfer them to a tray lined with baking paper and sprinkle with the extra crystallised ginger. Leave to set, then store in a tin.

Tip: Without the chocolate glaze, these ginger snaps make an excellent base for a cheesecake (e.g. Eggnog Cheesecake, page 83).

RUGELACH

Which bakery makes New York's very best rugelach? That is a hotly debated topic. What is clear is that this type of pastry, which comes from Israel, is very popular in the Big Apple. These small, hand-made crescents are available with a wide range of fillings.

Combine the flour and salt in a mixing bowl. Add the butter and cream cheese and rub in until the mixture holds together in crumbs. Stir in the egg yolk and vanilla extract.

Divide the dough into four portions. Shape each into a ball and then flatten. Wrap the dough in plastic wrap and chill for at least 2 hours.

Preheat the oven to 180°C (350°F) and line two baking trays with baking paper. For the filling, very finely chop the walnuts, currants and chocolate by hand or in a food processor. Combine the sugar and cinnamon in a bowl and set aside.

Dust your benchtop with icing sugar, remove one portion of dough from the refrigerator and roll it out to a circle about 25 cm (10 inches) in diameter. Spread the dough with 2 Tbsp of the jam and sprinkle with a little of the sugar and cinnamon, followed by a quarter of the filling.

Cut the dough into 12 wedges using a pizza cutter or sharp knife. Roll up the slices, starting from the widest point. Shape into crescents and transfer to the baking trays. Repeat with the remaining dough and filling. Bake the rugelach until golden brown, about 25 minutes.

INGREDIENTS

Makes about 48

240 g (8½ oz) plain flour
¼ tsp salt
230 g (8 oz) cold butter, diced
230 g (8 oz) cold cream cheese
1 egg yolk
1 tsp vanilla extract

For the filling:
120 g (4¼ oz) walnuts
75 g (2½ oz) currants
50 g (1¾ oz) dark chocolate
100 g (3½ oz) brown sugar
3 tsp ground cinnamon
About 225 g (8 oz) apricot jam

Also:
Icing (confectioners') sugar
for rolling

PINWHEEL COOKIES

If cutting cookies is not one of your favourite Christmas baking activities, this is just the recipe for you! The two types of dough for these cookies are simply rolled up together and sliced. Festively wrapped pinwheel cookies make lovely little Christmas or Advent gifts.

INGREDIENTS

Makes about 40

150 g (5½ oz) butter, at room temperature
100 g (3½ oz) icing (confectioners') sugar
200 g (7 oz) plain flour
2 Tbsp cocoa powder
¼ tsp vanilla extract
½ tsp peppermint extract (or a few drops of peppermint oil)

Also:
1 egg yolk
1 Tbsp milk

Beat the butter in a bowl until creamy, about 3 minutes. Add the icing sugar and a pinch of salt and beat for 2 minutes, until light and fluffy. Sift the flour over the top and fold into the mixture. Transfer half of the dough to another bowl.

Add the cocoa powder and vanilla extract to one half of the dough and the peppermint extract to the other. Combine well.

Roll out each half of the dough between two sheets of baking paper to make a rectangle about 15 x 30 cm (6 x 12 inches). Make the dark rectangle slightly thinner and larger. Whisk the egg yolk with the milk, then lightly brush over the dark rectangle. Place the light rectangle on top, then tightly roll up the dough, starting from the shorter side. Trim the ends and cut the roll in half. Wrap the two dough rolls in plastic wrap and freeze for 1 hour.

Preheat the oven to 180°C (350°F) and line two baking trays with baking paper. Cut the dough into slices about 5 mm (½ inch) thick and place on the baking trays. Bake the cookies for about 12 minutes. Transfer to a wire rack and leave to cool.

SNICKERDOODLES

It is not quite clear how snickerdoodles got their name. According to one theory, the name is derived from the German word 'schnecke', meaning 'snail', whereas another says it is simply a made-up word. What we do know is that these cookies are rolled in cinnamon sugar before baking, which makes smell incredibly delicious in the oven and gives them a particularly crunchy texture.

Combine the flour with the baking powder, bicarbonate of soda and salt in a bowl and set aside. Beat the butter and sugars in a mixing bowl until creamy. Add the egg and continue to whisk for 1 minute. Stir in the vanilla extract and fold in the flour mixture in two batches. Transfer the dough to the refrigerator to rest for 1 hour.

Preheat the oven to 180°C (350°F) and line two baking trays with baking paper. Combine the extra sugar and cinnamon in a bowl and set aside. Shape the dough into walnut-sized balls between your hands. Roll the dough balls in the cinnamon sugar, gently press to flatten, then transfer to the trays. Bake until golden brown, about 10 minutes, then transfer to a wire rack to cool.

INGREDIENTS

Makes about 24

180 g (6 oz) plain flour
¾ tsp baking powder
½ tsp bicarbonate of soda
(baking soda)
¼ tsp salt
110 g (3¾ oz) butter, at
room temperature
75 g (2½ oz) raw sugar
50 g (1¾ oz) dark brown sugar
1 egg
½ tsp vanilla extract

Also:
1 Tbsp raw sugar
½ Tbsp ground cinnamon

GINGERBREAD PEOPLE

These little figures made out of sweet, spiced dough have a long history. One popular fairytale tells the story of an old couple who baked a gingerbread man, only to have him escape from their oven. Decorating gingerbread people with icing is great fun and is easy to do using ready-made icing pens. Alternatively, combine some icing (confectioners') sugar with just enough milk to make a thick glaze. Transfer the mixture to a piping bag with a very small nozzle and get creative!

INGREDIENTS

Makes about 25–30

210 g (7½ oz) plain flour
1¼ tsp ground ginger
½ tsp ground cinnamon
¼ tsp ground cloves
¼ tsp freshly grated
nutmeg
½ tsp bicarbonate of soda
(baking soda)
85 g (3 oz) butter, at
room temperature
90 g (3¼ oz) raw sugar
1 egg yolk
50 g (1¾ oz) molasses

For decorating:
1 white icing pen

Also:
Flour for dusting

Sift the flour with the spices, bicarbonate of soda and pinch of salt into a bowl and set aside. Beat the butter in a separate bowl until creamy, about 3 minutes. Gradually add the sugar and beat for another 2 minutes. Stir in the egg yolk and molasses. Add the flour mixture in several batches and mix to a smooth dough. Cover and rest in the refrigerator for at least 2 hours, preferably overnight.

Preheat the oven to 180°C (350°F) and line two baking trays with baking paper. Lightly dust your benchtop with flour and roll out the dough about 3 mm (⅛ inch) thick. Using a cutter, cut the dough into people shapes and transfer to the trays. Bake for 8–12 minutes, depending on size. Remove from the oven and leave to cool on a wire rack.

Decorate with icing.

CHEESECAKE COOKIES

There's nothing better than a deliciously moist New York cheesecake, and these cookie-sized versions are utter delights too. The indulgent topping is an absolute must. Use cranberry or apricot jam instead of morello cherry jam, if you prefer.

Beat the cream cheese in a bowl. Add the butter and sugar and continue to beat until creamy. Stir in the egg and vanilla extract. Combine the flour with the bicarbonate of soda and salt in a bowl, then fold into the cream cheese mixture. Cover and rest in the refrigerator overnight.

Preheat the oven to 180°C (350°F) and line a baking tray with baking paper. Finely crush the cookies, transfer the crumbs to a small bowl and set aside.

Take small portions of the dough and shape into balls with a diameter of about 2.5 cm (1 inch). Roll the balls in the cookie crumbs, then transfer to the tray. Use the handle of a wooden spoon to make a small depression in the centre of each cookie and fill it with jam.

Bake the cookies for about 12 minutes.

INGREDIENTS

Makes about 48

220 g (7¾ oz) cream cheese,
at room temperature
120 g (4¼ oz) butter, at
room temperature
130 g (4½ oz) raw sugar
1 egg
1 tsp vanilla extract
250 g (9 oz) plain flour
1 tsp bicarbonate of soda
(baking soda)
¼ tsp salt
12 chocolate cookies (you
can use the cookies from
the Peanut butter sandwich
cookies on page 41)
A few Tbsp morello
cherry jam

APPLE & OAT COOKIES

Cookies made out of traditional rolled oats are particularly popular during the pre-Christmas season. Toasting the oats for the dough gives the cookies a deeper, nuttier flavour. Our tip: these cookies taste even better on the day after baking!

INGREDIENTS

Makes about 30

150 g (5½ oz) rolled oats
½ apple
1 tsp lemon juice
60 g (2¼ oz) butter, at
room temperature
150 g (5½ oz) dark brown sugar
50 g (1¾ oz) raw sugar
90 g (3¼ oz) apple purée
1 egg
1 Tbsp golden syrup
1 tsp vanilla extract
150 g (5½ oz) plain flour
1 tsp ground cinnamon
¼ tsp ground cardamom
¼ tsp freshly grated nutmeg
½ tsp baking powder
½ tsp bicarbonate of soda
(baking soda)
½ tsp salt
80 g (2¾ oz) walnuts,
finely chopped

For the icing:
1 white icing pen

Preheat the oven to 180°C (350°F) and line two baking trays with baking paper. Toast the oats in a small frying pan over medium heat. Remove from the heat and set aside to cool. Dice the apple very finely and drizzle with the lemon juice.

Beat the butter and sugars in a bowl for about 3 minutes, until creamy. Whisk the apple purée, egg, golden syrup and vanilla extract together and add to the butter mixture. Beat until light and fluffy, about 1 minute. Combine the flour with the spices, baking powder, bicarbonate of soda and salt, and fold in with a wooden spoon. Stir in the walnuts, oats and diced apple.

Use a tablespoon to drop the batter onto the trays in small heaps. Bake until golden brown, about 13–15 minutes. Remove from the oven and leave to cool on a wire rack.

Decorate with icing once completely cool.

HOLIDAY CAKES

PIES, CUPCAKES & CO.

GRAPE PIE

You should always take the time to taste one of the city's delicious pies whenever you're lucky enough to be in New York. It should be easy enough to find one, as any good bakery worth its salt (or sugar) will have a good selection. The best-known pie is probably the classic apple pie, which even has its own holiday in the US: National Apple Pie Day is celebrated on 13 May.

For the pastry, combine the flour, sugar, salt and cinnamon in a mixing bowl. Add the butter and rub in until the mixture holds together in pea-sized crumbs. Slowly add enough water to make a smooth dough. Press the dough to flatten, wrap it in plastic wrap and refrigerate for 2 hours.

For the filling, place the grapes in a saucepan and simmer over medium heat for about 8 minutes. Add the remaining ingredients and cook, stirring, until thickened.

Preheat the oven to 200°C (400°F). Divide the dough into two portions, making one a little bigger than the other. Lightly dust your benchtop with flour. Roll out the larger dough portion to line a 22 cm (8½ inch) fluted pie dish, leaving a little to overhang the edges. Fold the edges down and shape them to your liking, for example by fluting with your fingers or pressing with a fork to create a pattern. Refrigerate the dough in the pie dish. Meanwhile, roll out the remaining dough and cut out stars or other shapes.

Spread the filling into the pie shell and top with the pastry shapes. Whisk the egg yolk with the cream and brush over the pastry. Bake for 20 minutes, then reduce the oven temperature to 180°C (350°F) and bake for another 20 minutes.

Tip: Serve with a scoop of vanilla ice cream.

INGREDIENTS

Makes one 22 cm (8½ inch) pie

For the pastry:
280 g (10 oz) plain flour
1 Tbsp raw sugar
½ tsp salt
1 pinch ground cinnamon
180 g (6 oz) cold butter, diced
About 6 Tbsp ice-cold water

For the filling:
1 kg (2 lb 4 oz) black grapes
100 g (3½ oz) raw sugar
2 tsp lemon juice
3½ Tbsp cornflour
1 tsp grated orange zest
1 pinch ground cloves

Also:
Flour for dusting
1 egg yolk
1 Tbsp single (pure) cream

GINGERBREAD COOKIE CUPS

INGREDIENTS

Makes about 36

125 g (4½ oz) butter, at
room temperature
120 g (4¼ oz) dark brown sugar
60 g (2¼ oz) molasses
1 egg
1 tsp grated orange zest
260 g (9¼ oz) plain flour
2 tsp cocoa powder
½ tsp bicarbonate of soda
(baking soda)
1½ tsp ground ginger
1 tsp ground cinnamon
¼ tsp ground cloves

For the filling:
75 g (2½ oz) dark chocolate,
coarsely grated
150 ml (5 fl oz) single (pure)
cream
200 g (7 oz) cream cheese,
at room temperature
100 g (3½ oz) icing
(confectioners') sugar
¼ tsp ground ginger
1 Tbsp orange juice

Also:
Butter and flour for the tin
Ground cinnamon

Beat the butter and dark brown sugar in a bowl until creamy, about 3 minutes. Stir in the molasses, egg and orange zest and continue to beat for 1 minute. Combine the flour, cocoa powder, bicarbonate of soda, spices and a pinch of salt in a separate bowl. Add to the butter and egg mixture and continue stirring to make a smooth dough. Leave to rest in the refrigerator for about 1 hour.

Preheat the oven to 180°C (350°F). Butter a mini muffin tray and dust with flour. Shape the dough into 36 walnut-sized balls. Press the balls flat between your palms and use them to line the muffin holes. Bake the cookie cups for 10 minutes, being careful not to brown them. Remove from the oven and, if necessary, press the hot cookie cups further into the moulds to make a larger hollow in the middle. Place 1 tsp grated chocolate into each hollow and allow to melt. Use a pastry brush to spread the melted chocolate over the insides of the cookie cups. Leave them to cool.

For the filling, whisk the cream until stiff. Whisk the remaining ingredients in a bowl until creamy. Fold in the whipped cream in three batches. Transfer the mixture to a piping bag and pipe inside the cookie cups. Serve dusted with a little cinnamon.

COFFEE CAKE WITH FROSTED CRANBERRIES

Make the frosted cranberries a day ahead: bring 30 ml (1 fl oz) water and 25 g (1 oz) sugar to the boil. Take off the heat once the sugar has dissolved. Gently toss the cranberries in the syrup, then remove and set aside to dry a little on a fine-meshed cooling rack or similar for 1 hour. Gently toss in the remaining sugar and leave to dry overnight on baking paper.

Preheat the oven to 160°C (320°F). Butter two 20 cm (8 inch) springform cake tins and dust with cocoa powder. Melt the butter in the hot coffee. Thoroughly combine the cocoa powder with the flour, sugars, baking powder, bicarbonate of soda and salt in a mixing bowl. Whisk the eggs with the buttermilk and vanilla extract in a separate bowl. Add the wet ingredients to the dry in batches, alternating between the buttermilk mixture and the coffee mixture.

Divide the batter evenly between the tins. Bake for 35–40 minutes, using a toothpick to test for doneness. Leave the cakes to cool in the tins for 10 minutes, then remove from the tins and set aside to cool completely on wire racks. If necessary, use a large serrated knife to level the bases.

For the cranberry cream, add the cranberries, sugar, a pinch of salt and 80 ml (2½ fl oz) water to a saucepan. Bring to the boil, then simmer for 5 minutes. Remove from the heat, then purée and set aside to cool.

Beat the butter in a bowl until creamy, about 3 minutes. Add the cream cheese, icing sugar and cranberry purée, mixing until smooth.

Spread one of the cake bases with one-third of the cranberry cream. Place the other cake on top. Spread the cranberry cream thinly all over the cake and refrigerate for 15 minutes. Carefully glaze the cake with the remaining cranberry cream. Decorate the top with the frosted cranberries.

INGREDIENTS

Makes one 20 cm (8 inch) cake

100 g (3½ oz) butter, diced
240 ml (8 fl oz) hot coffee
100 g (3½ oz) cocoa powder
200 g (7 oz) plain flour
180 g (6 oz) raw sugar
120 g (4¼ oz) brown sugar
2 tsp baking powder
1½ tsp bicarbonate of soda
(baking soda)
¼ tsp salt
3 eggs
240 ml (8 fl oz) buttermilk
2 tsp vanilla extract

For the cranberry cream:
300 g (10½ oz) cranberries
40 g (1½ oz) raw sugar
300 g (10½ oz) butter, at
room temperature
150 g (5½ oz) cream cheese,
at room temperature
120 g (4¼ oz) icing
(confectioners') sugar

For the frosted cranberries:
About 100 g (3½ oz) raw sugar
70 g (2½ oz) cranberries

Also:
Butter and cocoa powder
for the tins

CHOCOLATE, PECAN & SALTED CARAMEL SQUARES

INGREDIENTS

Makes about 15 pieces

125 g (4½ oz) plain flour
80 g (2¾ oz) butter, melted
60 g (2¼ oz) icing
(confectioners') sugar
¼ tsp salt

For the chocolate layer:
100 g (3½ oz) plain flour
75 g (2½ oz) raw sugar
50 g (1¾ oz) dark brown sugar
25 g (1 oz) cocoa powder
½ tsp baking powder
¼ tsp bicarbonate of soda
(baking soda)
100 g (3½ oz) butter, melted
2 eggs
1 tsp vanilla extract
70 g (2½ oz) dark chocolate,
chopped
30 g (1 oz) pecans, chopped

For the caramel layer:
100 g (3½ oz) raw sugar
1 Tbsp maple syrup
10 g (¼ oz) cold butter
60 ml (2 fl oz) single (pure) cream
½ tsp vanilla extract
½ tsp salt
30 g (1 oz) dark chocolate, chopped
70 g pecans, chopped

Preheat the oven to 180°C (350°F). Line a 20 x 30 cm (8 x 12 inch) cake tin with baking paper. Combine the flour, melted butter, icing sugar and salt in a mixing bowl and rub together. Set aside 25 g (1 oz) of the crumble mixture. Press the remainder into the tin and bake until golden brown, about 10 minutes. Remove from the oven and leave to cool for 20 minutes.

For the chocolate layer, combine the flour, raw sugar, brown sugar, cocoa powder, baking powder, bicarbonate of soda and a generous pinch of salt in a mixing bowl. Whisk the butter, eggs and vanilla in another bowl. Stir into the dry ingredients, then fold in the chocolate and nuts. Spread over the base and bake for about 25 minutes. Remove from the oven and leave to cool briefly.

For the topping, put the sugar, maple syrup and 4 Tbsp water in a saucepan and caramelise over medium heat for about 12 minutes. Stir in the butter and then the cream, vanilla extract and salt. Drizzle over the chocolate layer and then top with the chopped chocolate and nuts. Sprinkle the reserved crumble over the top and bake for 5 minutes. Leave to cool completely, then cut into squares.

HOLIDAY BUNDT CAKE

Preheat the oven to 170°C (340°F). Butter a 22 cm (8½ inch) ring tin and dust with flour. Finely chop the apricots, place in a bowl and drizzle with bourbon. Spread the pecans on a baking tray and roast in the oven for about 6 minutes. Cool slightly, then finely chop 100 g (3½ oz) of the pecans.

Combine the flour with the baking powder, spices, bicarbonate of soda and salt in a mixing bowl. Whisk the buttermilk, molasses, vanilla extract, orange zest and grated ginger in a separate bowl. Add the oil and both types of sugar to a third bowl and whisk until light and fluffy, about 3 minutes. Whisk in the eggs, one at a time, for 1 minute each, then stir in the flour mixture and buttermilk mixture alternately in two batches each. Fold in the apricots, chopped pecans and the cranberries.

Transfer the batter to the tin and bake for 60–70 minutes. Use a toothpick to test for doneness. Remove the cake from the oven and wrap a damp tea towel around the base of the tin. Set aside for about 10 minutes, then invert the cake onto a wire rack and leave to cool completely.

For the icing, place the icing sugar in a bowl. Add the orange juice and stir until smooth. Drizzle the icing over the cake so that it runs down the sides. Garnish with the reserved pecans and orange zest.

INGREDIENTS

Makes one 22 cm (8½ inch) cake

100 g (3½ oz) dried apricots
3 Tbsp bourbon (or orange juice)
150 g (5½ oz) pecans
360 g (12¾ oz) plain flour
1½ tsp baking powder
1½ tsp ground cinnamon
1 tsp ground allspice
½ tsp ground cardamom
½ tsp ground cloves
½ tsp freshly grated nutmeg
½ tsp bicarbonate of soda
(baking soda)
1 tsp salt
240 ml (8 fl oz) buttermilk
100 g (3½ oz) molasses
2 tsp vanilla extract
Grated zest of 1 orange
2 tsp grated fresh ginger
240 ml (8 fl oz) coconut oil
150 g (5½ oz) brown sugar
100 g (3½ oz) raw sugar
4 eggs
30 g (1 oz) dried cranberries

For the icing:
100 g (3½ oz) icing
(confectioners') sugar
30 ml (1 fl oz) orange juice
1 Tbsp grated orange zest

Also:
Butter and flour for the tin

RED VELVET CHRISTMAS CUPCAKES

INGREDIENTS

Makes 12

130 g (4½ oz) plain flour
1½ Tbsp cocoa powder
¼ tsp baking powder
¼ tsp salt
60 g (2¼ oz) butter, at
room temperature
130 g (4½ oz) raw sugar
1 egg
120 ml (4 fl oz) buttermilk,
at room temperature
1½ Tbsp red food colouring
(or beetroot powder)
1 tsp vanilla extract
¼ tsp bicarbonate of soda
(baking soda)
1 tsp apple cider vinegar

For the cream:
120 ml (4 fl oz) milk
20 g (¾ oz) plain flour
100 g (3½ oz) butter, at
room temperature
1 tsp vanilla sugar
60 g (2¼ oz) icing
(confectioners') sugar

Also:
Paper baking cups
Star-shaped sprinkles

For the cream, pour the milk into a saucepan and whisk in the flour and a pinch of salt. Bring to the boil, stirring constantly, then simmer until thickened to a custard. Remove from the heat, cover the surface with plastic wrap to prevent a skin from forming and leave to cool completely.

Beat the butter, vanilla sugar and icing sugar until creamy, about 3 minutes. Gradually whisk in the custard until the mixture is fluffy. Cover and refrigerate until needed.

Preheat the oven to 180°C (350°F). Line 12 holes of a muffin tray with paper baking cups. Combine the flour with the cocoa powder, baking powder and salt in a mixing bowl and set aside. Beat the butter in a separate bowl until creamy, about 3 minutes, then gradually add the sugar. Add the egg and beat for 1 minute. Combine the buttermilk with the food colouring and vanilla extract. Mix the flour mixture and the buttermilk mixture alternately into the butter mixture in two batches, stirring constantly. Combine the bicarbonate of soda and vinegar in a small bowl and fold into the batter. Divide the batter among the baking cups and bake for 15–18 minutes. Remove from the oven and set aside to cool completely.

Transfer the cream into a piping bag with a wide nozzle. Pipe the topping onto the cooled cupcakes and decorate with the star-shaped sprinkles.

GINGERBREAD PEAR CAKE

Prepare the pears a day ahead: combine the sugar with 1.5 litres (52 fl oz) water in a saucepan. Split the vanilla bean lengthwise and scrape the seeds into the saucepan. Add the vanilla bean, ginger, cinnamon sticks, star anise and cardamom. Bring to the boil, then reduce the heat to low and simmer until the syrup has reduced by half. Peel the pears, keeping the stems on. Transfer the peeled pears to a bowl, cover with the syrup and marinate overnight in the refrigerator.

Preheat the oven to 170°C (340°F) and line a 30 cm (12 inch) loaf tin with baking paper. Remove the pears from the syrup and leave to drain thoroughly.

Combine the flour, cinnamon, baking powder, bicarbonate of soda, salt and spices in a bowl and set aside. Beat the butter and brown sugar in another bowl until creamy, about 3 minutes. Add the egg and beat for 1 minute to combine. Stir in the molasses, honey, grated ginger and vanilla extract. Fold in the flour mixture and yoghurt alternately in two batches.

Transfer the batter to the loaf tin. Push the pears into the batter, leaving the stems sticking out the top. Combine the raw sugar and ground ginger, and sprinkle over the top of the batter. Bake until golden brown, about 60–70 minutes. Use a toothpick to test for doneness. Remove the cake from the oven and leave it to cool. Dust with icing sugar and serve.

INGREDIENTS

Makes one 30 cm (12 inch) loaf

230 g (8 oz) plain flour
1½ tsp ground cinnamon
1 tsp baking powder
¼ tsp bicarbonate of soda
(baking soda)
¼ tsp salt
¼ tsp ground allspice
¼ tsp ground cloves
¼ tsp freshly grated nutmeg
110 g (3¾ oz) butter, at
room temperature
100 g (3½ oz) brown sugar
1 egg
70 g (2½ oz) molasses
40 g (1½ oz) honey
1½ Tbsp grated fresh ginger
½ tsp vanilla extract
150 g (5½ oz) plain yoghurt
1½ Tbsp raw sugar
½ tsp ground ginger

For the pears:
140 g (5 oz) raw sugar
1 vanilla bean
1 cm (½ inch) piece ginger
2 cinnamon sticks
2 star anise
6 cardamom pods
4–5 small pears

Also:
Icing (confectioners') sugar

UPSIDE-DOWN CAKE
WITH CRANBERRIES

Upside-down cakes were invented around 1925, at a time when convenience products such as sliced pineapple in tins first appeared in supermarkets. Tinned pineapple and cocktail cherries were frequently used for this classic cake. The fruit pieces are arranged in the base of the tin and then, once the cake is turned out, they make a beautiful topping and keep the cake deliciously moist.

INGREDIENTS

Makes one 23 cm (9 inch) cake

1 orange
150 g (5½ oz) cranberries
200 g (7 oz) plain flour
40 g (1½ oz) fine polenta
2 tsp baking powder
¼ tsp bicarbonate of soda
(baking soda)
¼ tsp salt
1 pinch ground cinnamon
160 ml (5¼ fl oz) buttermilk
1 tsp vanilla extract
1 tsp almond extract
100 g (3½ oz) butter, at room
temperature
120 g (4¼ oz) raw sugar
2 eggs

Also:
1 Tbsp butter
70 g (2½ oz) brown sugar

Preheat the oven to 180°C (350°F) and line the outside of a 23 cm (9 inch) spring-form cake tin with foil to prevent any batter from leaking. Grease the inside of the tin with butter and sprinkle with the brown sugar.

Wash the orange under hot water and pat dry. Grate the zest and set aside. Halve the orange, juice one half and transfer the juice to a small saucepan together with the cranberries. Bring to the boil, then reduce the heat and simmer over medium heat for about 4 minutes. Remove from the heat and set aside to cool.

Peel the remaining orange half, removing all of the bitter white pith. Cut three thin slices, then cut each slice in half. Arrange on the base of the cake tin and cover with the cranberry mixture.

Combine the flour, polenta, baking powder, bicarbonate of soda, salt and cinnamon in a bowl. Whisk the buttermilk, orange zest and vanilla and almond extract in another bowl. Beat the butter and sugar until creamy, about 3 minutes. Add the eggs one at a time, beating for about 1 minute each. Use a wooden spoon to fold in the flour mixture and buttermilk mixture in two batches, alternating between the two.

Spread the batter on top of the cranberries and bake for about 50 minutes. Use a toothpick to test for doneness. Leave to cool in the tin for 15 minutes before inverting the cake onto a wire rack and leaving it to cool completely.

Tip: This is delicious served with cream that has been whipped with a pinch of cinnamon.

EGGNOG CHEESECAKE

Preheat the oven to 180°C (350°F) and line the outside of a 23 cm (9 inch) spring-form cake tin with two layers of foil to prevent any batter from escaping. Finely crush the biscuits and combine with the melted butter, brown sugar and cinnamon in a bowl. Press firmly onto the base of the tin and bake for 10 minutes. Remove from the oven and set aside to cool.

For the filling, beat the cream cheese in a bowl until fluffy, then stir in the crème fraîche and butter. Add the sugar, cornflour, nutmeg and cinnamon. Stir in the rum and cognac. Finally add the eggs and egg yolks, one at a time. Pour the mixture over the base and place the spring-form tin inside a roasting tin. Add enough boiling water to come 2.5 cm (1 inch) up the side of the springform tin.

Bake the cheesecake for 45 minutes, then reduce the oven to 160°C (320°F) and continue baking for another 25 minutes. The cheesecake should not be fully set yet. Turn off the oven and leave the cheesecake inside to cool for 1 hour, keeping the oven door slightly ajar. Remove the cheesecake from the oven, take off the foil and set the cheesecake aside in its tin to cool completely on a wire rack. Cover with foil and refrigerate for at least 4 hours, ideally overnight, before removing the cheesecake from the tin.

Whip the cream until stiff, sweeten with icing sugar and spread on top of the cheesecake. Dust with nutmeg and cinnamon, and grate the white chocolate over the top.

INGREDIENTS

Makes one 23 cm (9 inch) cake

160 g (5½ oz) shortbread
biscuits (or use the Ginger
Snaps on page 44)
80 g (2¾ oz) butter, melted
2 Tbsp brown sugar
¼ tsp ground cinnamon

For the filling:
900 g (2 lb) cream cheese,
at room temperature
250 g (9 oz) crème fraîche,
at room temperature
25 g (1 oz) butter, softened
200 g (7 oz) raw sugar
2 Tbsp cornflour
1½ tsp freshly grated
nutmeg
1 tsp ground cinnamon
3 Tbsp dark rum
2 Tbsp cognac
4 eggs
2 egg yolks

Also:
200 ml (7 fl oz) single
(pure) cream
1 Tbsp icing (confectioners')
sugar, to taste
A little freshly grated nutmeg
and ground cinnamon
25 g (1 oz) white chocolate

CHOCOLATE FRUIT CAKE

INGREDIENTS

Makes one 23 cm (9 inch) cake

100 g (3½ oz) each dried
apricots, dates, figs, prunes
and raisins
140 g (5 oz) dried cherries
1 vanilla bean
100 ml (3½ fl oz) bourbon or rum
100 ml (3½ fl oz) hot water
160 g (5½ oz) plain flour
2 tsp cocoa powder
1 tsp baking powder
½ tsp ground cinnamon
120 g (4¼ oz) each pistachios,
pecans and almonds,
finely chopped
100 g (3½ oz) dark chocolate
(70% cocoa), coarsely chopped
75 g (2½ oz) dried cranberries,
chopped
100 g (3½ oz) butter, at
room temperature
100 g (3½ oz) dark brown sugar
2 eggs

For the topping:
Blanched almonds
Mixed dried fruit to taste
2 Tbsp sugar
3 Tbsp apricot jam

Also:
Butter for the tin

Coarsely chop the apricots, dates, figs and prunes and transfer the chopped fruit to a heatproof bowl together with the raisins and cherries. Split the vanilla bean lengthwise and scrape out the seeds. Add the vanilla bean to the dried fruit and set the seeds aside. Warm the bourbon and add to the fruit together with the hot water. Marinate for 1 hour, stirring occasionally. Drain the fruit, reserving the liquid. Discard the vanilla bean.

Preheat the oven to 160°C (320°F). Butter a 23 cm (9 inch) spring-form cake tin and line with baking paper.

Combine the flour, cocoa powder, baking powder, cinnamon and a pinch of salt in a bowl. Stir in the nuts, chocolate and cranberries. Beat the butter and sugar in another bowl until creamy, about 3 minutes. Add the eggs, one at a time, and stir in the vanilla seeds. Use a wooden spoon to fold in first the soaked dried fruit and then the nut, fruit and flour mixture. Transfer the batter to the prepared tin, level the top and garnish with almonds.

Bake the cake for 60–75 minutes. Cover with baking paper after about half the baking time. Remove from the oven and set aside to cool completely. Coarsely chop the extra mixed dried fruit and sprinkle on top of the cake. Heat about 200 ml (7 fl oz) of the reserved soaking liquid over low heat and stir in the sugar and jam. Drizzle the cake with the glaze before serving.

MINI CRANBERRY PIES

Feel free to experiment with different fruits in these pretty little delicacies. Try using blueberries or raspberries instead of the cranberries, for example. They are lovely served with a pot of coffee and enjoyed with friends.

Combine the flour, sugar, pecans, salt and cinnamon in a bowl. Add the butter and chocolate and rub in quickly until the mixture resembles coarse breadcrumbs. Whisk the egg, add to the dough and knead until smooth. Wrap in plastic wrap and leave to rest in the refrigerator for 30 minutes.

For the filling, combine the cranberries and sugar in a saucepan. Wash the mandarins under hot water and pat dry. Grate the zest and add it to the pan. Bring to the boil, then reduce the heat and simmer over medium heat for about 3 minutes. Meanwhile, juice the mandarins. Combine the juice with the cornflour and add it to the cranberries with a pinch of salt. Simmer for another 1 minute, then remove from the heat and set aside to cool.

Preheat the oven to 200°C (400°F) and lightly butter a muffin tray. Roll out the dough about 4 mm (³/₁₆ inch) thick on a lightly floured surface. Use a cookie cutter to cut out 12 circles, 5 cm (2 inches) each. Line the muffin holes with the dough and spoon in the cranberry filling. Cut another 12 circles, about 6 cm (2½ inches), out of the remaining dough. Cut a small heart shape out of the centre of each circle, then place on top of the pies. Whisk the egg yolk until smooth with 1 Tbsp water and brush over the pies. Bake for 12–14 minutes, until golden brown.

INGREDIENTS

Makes 12

350 g (12 oz) plain flour
120 g (4¼ oz) raw sugar
3 Tbsp ground pecans (or ground almonds)
¼ tsp salt
¼ tsp ground cinnamon
150 g (5½ oz) cold butter, diced
50 g (1¾ oz) white chocolate, finely grated
1 egg

For the filling:
400 g (14 oz) cranberries
110 g (3¾ oz) raw sugar
2 mandarins
1 Tbsp cornflour

Also:
Butter for the tin
Flour for dusting
1 egg yolk for glazing

CHRISTMAS BREAKFAST

BREADS, MUFFINS & BUNS

BANANA PECAN WAFFLES

These waffles can be easily prepared the evening before, just like overnight oats. The batter can then prove in the refrigerator overnight, and your fluffy waffles will draw everyone towards the breakfast table in no time in the morning.

INGREDIENTS

Makes about 8

250 g (9 oz) plain flour
2 Tbsp ground pecans
(or ground almonds)
2 Tbsp brown sugar
1½ tsp dried yeast
½ tsp salt
½ tsp ground cinnamon
50 g (1¾ oz) butter, melted
1 Tbsp honey
2 tsp vanilla extract
330 ml (11¼ fl oz) buttermilk
2 eggs, separated
1 very ripe banana, mashed

For the topping:
2–3 bananas
About 80 g (2¾ oz) pecans
Maple syrup

Also:
Oil or butter for greasing
the waffle iron

Combine the flour, pecans, sugar, yeast, salt and cinnamon in a mixing bowl and mix well. Whisk the butter, honey and vanilla extract into the buttermilk. Pour into the flour mixture and mix well.

Cover the bowl and leave the batter to prove overnight in the refrigerator or for 2 hours in a warm place.

Beat the egg whites until stiff and set aside. Whisk the egg yolks with the mashed banana and stir into the batter. Gently fold in the egg whites.

Preheat and grease the waffle iron. Cook the waffles in batches. Slice the bananas and toast the pecans in a frying pan. Serve the waffles topped with pecans and sliced banana, drizzled with maple syrup.

BABKA WITH CINNAMON & WALNUTS

Thoroughly mix the flour, sugar, yeast, vanilla sugar and salt in a mixing bowl. Whisk the egg and egg yolk into the milk and stir into the dry ingredients. Knead the dough in a food processor or using the dough hook of an electric mixer. Gradually incorporate the butter. Transfer the dough to a lightly floured benchtop and knead with your hands until silky smooth, about 10 minutes. Do not add any additional flour at this step – the dough will lose its stickiness with kneading. Shape the dough into a ball, transfer to a large oiled bowl and cover with plastic wrap. Leave the dough to rise for 2 hours at room temperature or overnight in the refrigerator.

For the filling, cover the raisins with warm water and leave to soak for 15 minutes. Drain and set aside about a quarter of the soaked raisins in a bowl. Purée the rest together with the sugar, butter, cinnamon and salt.

Line a 24 cm (9½ inch) loaf tin with baking paper. Dust your benchtop with flour and roll the dough out to a rectangle about 25 x 35 cm (10 x 14 inches). Spread with the filling and sprinkle with the raisins and walnuts. Roll up, starting from the shorter side. Turn the roll seam side down and cut in half lengthwise with a sharp knife to make two long strands. Intertwine these two strands by first placing the strands in a cross pattern and then twisting the ends around each other. Keep the filling side up. Transfer the plaited dough to the loaf tin, cover with a tea towel and leave to rise at room temperature for about 1 hour.

Preheat the oven to 180°C (350°F). Bake the babka until golden brown, about 35 minutes. Check towards the end of the baking time and cover the tin with baking paper or foil if the babka browns too much on top.

For the glaze, mix the butter, milk, cinnamon, sugar and a pinch of salt in a bowl until smooth. Brush on top of the hot babka.

INGREDIENTS

Makes one 24 cm (9½ inch) loaf

260 g (9¼ oz) plain flour
40 g (1½ oz) raw sugar
1 tsp dried yeast
8 g (¼ oz) bourbon vanilla sugar
¼ tsp salt
1 egg
1 egg yolk
80 ml (2½ fl oz) milk
60 g (2¼ oz) butter, at room temperature, diced

For the filling:
250 g (9 oz) raisins
75 g (2½ oz) brown sugar
45 g (1½ oz) butter, at room temperature
1½ tsp ground cinnamon
½ tsp salt
70 g (2½ oz) walnuts, chopped

For the glaze:
50 g (1¾ oz) butter, melted
3 Tbsp milk
1 Tbsp ground cinnamon
65 g (2¼ oz) icing (confectioners') sugar

Also:
Flour for dusting
1 tsp oil for the bowl

APPLE CRUMBLE MUFFINS

Apple and cinnamon are the dream team that makes these muffins a memorable culinary experience. In New York, you can probably find thousands of muffin varieties, from sweet to savoury. They are a staple for New York breakfasts and taste best with a cup of freshly brewed hot coffee.

INGREDIENTS

Makes 12

180 g (6 oz) plain flour
1 tsp baking powder
1 tsp bicarbonate of soda
(baking soda)
1 tsp ground cinnamon
½ tsp salt
120 g (4¼ oz) brown sugar
60 g (2¼ oz) butter, melted
2 eggs
1½ tsp vanilla extract
1½ small apples, very
finely diced

For the crumble:
70 g (2½ oz) brown sugar
60 g (2¼ oz) plain flour
50 g (1¾ oz) rolled oats
1 tsp ground cinnamon
1 pinch freshly grated
nutmeg
50 g (1¾ oz) butter, melted
1 small apple, very finely diced

Also:
Butter and flour for the tin
(or paper baking cups)

Preheat the oven to 200°C (400°F). Butter a muffin tray and dust with flour or line the holes with paper baking cups. For the crumble, combine all of the ingredients except the apple in a bowl. Rub together with your fingers and then refrigerate.

Combine the flour with the baking powder, bicarbonate of soda, cinnamon and salt in a mixing bowl. Whisk the sugar, melted butter, eggs and vanilla extract in another bowl. Add to the dry ingredients and mix loosely with a wooden spoon. Fold in the diced apple and divide the batter among the muffin holes.

Toss the crumble with the diced apple and sprinkle on top of the batter, pressing it lightly. Bake the muffins for 10 minutes, reduce the oven to 180°C (350°F) and then bake for another 10 minutes. Leave the muffins to cool for 10 minutes, then remove from the tray and cool completely on a wire rack.

CHOCOLATE STICKY BUNS

Thoroughly combine the flour with the sugar, yeast, salt and nutmeg in a mixing bowl. Whisk the buttermilk with the egg yolks, butter and vanilla extract and add to the dry ingredients. Stir to combine, then knead the dough for 5 minutes. Cover and leave to rise at room temperature for 2 hours.

Make the caramel just before the dough is finished proving. Melt the butter in a saucepan over medium heat. Add the sugar, cream, honey and salt and bring to the boil. Cook over low heat until light brown, about 4 minutes, then remove from the heat. Stir in the chocolate hazelnut spread and vanilla extract. Spread a rectangular cake tin with half of the caramel and sprinkle with half of the flaked almonds. Set the remaining caramel aside.

Transfer the dough to a lightly floured benchtop. Gently press to flatten the dough, then roll out to a rectangle 30 x 50 cm (12 x 20 inches) and brush with three-quarters of the melted butter. Top with the chocolate hazelnut spread. Combine the sugar, cinnamon and a pinch of salt and sprinkle on top. Roll up the dough tightly from the long side and slice into pieces about 3 cm (1¼ inches) wide. Transfer the pieces, cut side up, to the tin and leave to rise for another 45 minutes.

Preheat the oven to 160°C (320°F). Bake the buns until golden brown, about 35 minutes. Remove from the oven and brush with the remaining caramel while still hot. Sprinkle with the remaining flaked almonds and leave to cool to lukewarm.

INGREDIENTS

Makes about 15

400 g (14 oz) plain flour
40 g (1½ oz) brown sugar
2 teaspoons dried yeast
1 tsp salt
1 pinch freshly grated nutmeg
200 ml (7 fl oz) buttermilk,
at room temperature
3 egg yolks
50 g (1¾ oz) butter, melted
1 tsp vanilla extract

For the caramel:
120 g (4¼ oz) butter
200 g (7 oz) raw sugar
240 ml (8 fl oz) single
(pure) cream
80 g (2¾ oz) honey
¼ tsp salt
2 Tbsp chocolate hazelnut
spread
½ tsp vanilla extract

For the filling:
75 g (2½ oz) butter, melted
About 300 g (10½ oz) chocolate
hazelnut spread
60 g (2¼ oz) brown sugar
1 tsp ground cinnamon

Also:
About 50 g (1¾ oz) flaked
almonds
Flour for dusting

CANDY CANE BREAD

INGREDIENTS

Makes one loaf

300 g (10½ oz) plain flour
30 g (1 oz) raw sugar
½ Tbsp dried yeast
½ tsp salt
50 g (1¾ oz) butter, melted
1 egg, lightly beaten
170 ml (5½ fl oz) lukewarm
milk

For the cranberry filling:
150 g (5½ oz) cranberries
30 g (1 oz) raw sugar
1 tsp lemon juice
15 g (½ oz) cornflour

For the cream cheese filling:
1 egg, lightly beaten
100 g (3½ oz) cream cheese,
at room temperature
2 Tbsp raw sugar
1 tsp vanilla extract

For the topping:
About 2 Tbsp milk
About 100 g (3½ oz) icing
(confectioners') sugar

Also:
Flour for dusting
1 egg yolk for glazing

Combine the flour, sugar, yeast and salt in a mixing bowl. Whisk the butter and egg into the milk and stir the mixture into the dry ingredients. Knead for about 5 minutes to make a soft dough. Cover and leave to rise at room temperature for 2 hours.

For the filling, combine the cranberries, sugar and lemon juice in a saucepan. Bring to the boil, then simmer over medium heat for 4 minutes. Sift the cornstarch into the cranberry mixture, whisk to combine and simmer for another 1 minute. Remove from the heat and set aside to cool.

For the cream cheese filling, whisk the egg with the remaining ingredients until smooth. Refrigerate until ready to use.

Dust your benchtop with flour and roll the dough out to a rectangle about 55 x 20 cm (22 x 8 inches). Transfer the dough to a sheet of baking paper, leaving about a quarter of the long side to overhang (this part will be bent to make the cane shape later). Use a sharp knife to cut 10 cm (4 inch) slits along the long side of the dough at 2 cm (¾ inch) intervals. Do this from both sides, leaving a 10 cm (4 inch) wide strip intact at the centre. Spread this centre strip first with the cream cheese filling and then with the cranberry filling. Set aside a small amount of cranberry filling for decorating the bread. Fold the cut strips diagonally across the filling, alternating between the left and the right sides, to make a plaited pattern. Bend the plait into a cane shape and slide it onto a baking tray, together with the baking paper. Brush the bread with the egg yolk and leave to rise for 30 minutes.

Preheat the oven to 180°C (350°F). Bake the candy cane bread for 35–40 minutes until golden brown. Remove from the oven and leave to cool completely.

Whisk the milk into the icing sugar until smooth, then drizzle over the bread in diagonal lines. Do the same with the reserved cranberry filling to create a red-and-white candy cane pattern.

BREAD PUDDING

Bread pudding has a very long tradition, and there are many sweet and savoury varieties in different countries. While it was originally nothing more than a way of using up stale bread, bread pudding has become a popular dessert in its own right. It is usually served sweet in the USA, but its savoury cousin is just as tasty.

Preheat the oven to 180°C (350°F). Butter a 21 cm (8¼ inch) ovenproof dish. Cut the bread into 3 cm (1¼ inch) cubes and spread evenly across the base of the dish.

Heat the milk in a saucepan together with half of the butter, 2 Tbsp of the sugar, the vanilla extract, cinnamon and a pinch of salt until the butter has melted. Leave to cool to lukewarm, then whisk in the eggs. Pour the mixture over the bread cubes and set aside briefly to allow the bread to soak up the liquid, turning the bread cubes once to ensure they are evenly moist.

Dot the remaining butter over the pudding and sprinkle with the flaked almonds. Combine the remaining sugar with the nutmeg and sprinkle on top. Bake for 35–40 minutes until the pudding has set but is still a little soft. Serve warm.

Tip: If you use plain challah or another fruit-free bread, you may want to add 1 handful of chocolate chips, raisins or thinly sliced apples to the dish before baking.

INGREDIENTS

Makes about 4 servings

3½ fruit buns (or challah, challah buns, brioche etc.)
300 ml (10½ fl oz) milk
50 g (1¾ oz) butter
3 Tbsp raw sugar
1 tsp vanilla extract
½ tsp ground cinnamon
3 eggs, lightly beaten
2 Tbsp flaked almonds
1 pinch freshly grated nutmeg

Also:
Butter for the tin

BUTTERMILK BREAKFAST PUFFS

Dunked into warm butter and sprinkled with cinnamon sugar, these breakfast puffs make an incredible start to the day. The airy dough is reminiscent of doughnuts, and given the size of these little cakes, one could be forgiven for mistaking them for doughnut holes. However, they are simply and quickly baked in a mini muffin tray rather than deep-fried. The puffs are best fresh out of the oven, but it's unlikely that anybody would be able to resist their delicious smell for long anyway.

INGREDIENTS

Makes about 24–30

180 g (6 oz) plain flour
1 tsp baking powder
½ tsp bicarbonate of soda
(baking soda)
½ tsp salt
¼ tsp freshly grated
nutmeg
100 g (3½ oz) raw sugar
80 g (2¾ oz) butter, at
room temperature
1 egg
1 tsp vanilla extract
120 ml (4 fl oz) buttermilk,
at room temperature

For coating:
80 g (2¾ oz) butter
100 g (3½ oz) raw sugar
1 Tbsp ground cinnamon

Also:
Butter and flour for the tin

Preheat the oven to 180°C (350°F). Butter a mini muffin tray and dust with flour. Combine the flour with the baking powder, bicarbonate of soda, salt and nutmeg in a mixing bowl. Beat the sugar and butter in a separate bowl until light and creamy, about 3 minutes. Add the egg and continue to beat for 1 minute. Stir in the vanilla extract. Add the buttermilk and the flour mixture alternately in two batches until just combined. Be careful not to overmix. Divide the batter among the muffin holes and bake for 15–20 minutes.

Meanwhile, melt the butter for the coating in a small saucepan and heat until lightly browned. Remove from the heat. Combine the sugar and cinnamon in a small bowl.

Remove the breakfast puffs from the oven and set aside to cool for 2 minutes. Dunk the tops into the browned butter and then sprinkle generously with the cinnamon sugar. These are best eaten fresh.

CINNAMON ROLL PANCAKES

Preheat the oven to 180°C (350°F) and line a baking tray with baking paper. Cut the pumpkin in half and discard the seeds. Place on the tray, cut side down, and roast until soft, about 40 minutes. Scrape out the pumpkin flesh with a spoon and mash finely. Measure out 300 g (10½ oz) of the pumpkin purée and leave to cool. Freeze the remainder or use it for another recipe (e.g. Pumpkin spice whoopie pies, page 31). (These steps do not apply if you use apple sauce instead of pumpkin.)

For the cinnamon butter, add all the ingredients to a mixing bowl with a pinch of salt and beat until creamy. Transfer to a piping bag with a small round nozzle (or to a freezer bag with a corner cut off). Set aside.

For the cream cheese icing, beat the cream cheese, icing sugar and maple syrup together. Add a little milk, if necessary, and mix until the icing has the desired consistency. Set aside.

Combine the flour, baking powder, salt, bicarbonate of soda and spices in a mixing bowl. Whisk the egg yolks with the buttermilk, brown sugar, orange zest, vinegar and pumpkin purée. Stir into the dry ingredients until just combined. Do not overmix. Beat the egg whites until stiff, then gently fold into the batter in two batches.

Melt a little oil in a frying pan over medium heat. Add about 2 Tbsp batter to the pan per pancake and cook for 1–2 minutes. Pipe the cinnamon butter on top of the pancake in a spiral pattern and cook for another 1–2 minutes. Turn the pancake and cook until golden brown. Stack four to five pancakes per serving and drizzle the top pancake with cream cheese icing.

INGREDIENTS

Makes about 8 servings

800 g (1 lb 12 oz) pumpkin
(or 300 g/10½ oz apple sauce)
400 g (14 oz) plain flour
2 tsp baking powder
½ tsp salt
¼ tsp bicarbonate of soda
(baking soda)
1 tsp ground cinnamon
1 tsp ground ginger
¼ tsp freshly grated nutmeg
1 pinch ground cloves
1 pinch ground allspice
2 eggs, separated
400 ml (14 fl oz) buttermilk
2 Tbsp brown sugar
1 tsp grated orange zest
2 tsp apple cider vinegar

For the cinnamon butter:
90 g (3¼ oz) very soft butter
60 g (2¼ oz) brown sugar
1½ Tbsp plain flour
2 tsp ground cinnamon

For the cream cheese icing:
80 g (2¾ oz) cream cheese
1½ tsp icing (confectioners')
sugar
1 tsp maple syrup
About 2 tsp milk

Also:
Oil (or butter) for frying

DATE NUT BREAD

Dates and nuts are the perfect ingredients for the Christmas season. However, this date nut bread brings variety to the breakfast table at any time during the colder months. If you want to make gifts out of this bread, why not bake it in cleaned, empty food tins? If so, reduce the baking time to about 40 minutes.

INGREDIENTS

Makes one 20 cm (8 inch) loaf

230 g (8 oz) dates,
coarsely chopped
100 g (3½ oz) dark brown
sugar
60 g (2¼ oz) butter, diced
1 tsp bicarbonate of soda
(baking soda)
½ tsp salt
250 ml (9 fl oz) hot coffee
(or water)
1 egg
1 tsp vanilla extract
1 Tbsp rum, to taste
250 g (9 oz) plain flour
½ tsp ground cinnamon
½ tsp baking powder
120 g (4¼ oz) walnuts,
coarsely chopped

Also:
Cream cheese for spreading

Preheat the oven to 180°C (350°F) and line a 20 cm (8 inch) loaf tin with baking paper. Combine the dates with the sugar, butter, bicarbonate of soda and salt in a mixing bowl. Add the coffee and leave to soak for 15 minutes.

Whisk the egg with the vanilla extract and rum in a small bowl. Combine the flour with the cinnamon and baking powder. Add the egg and flour mixtures to the date mixture, stir briefly to combine and then fold in the walnuts.

Transfer the batter to the loaf tin and bake for about 50 minutes. Check after 30 minutes and cover with foil if the top is browning too quickly. Use a toothpick to test for doneness. Remove from the oven and leave to cool. Slice and serve with cream cheese.

APPLE CIDER DOUGHNUTS

New Yorkers actually don't mind queuing, provided they find the city's very best doughnuts at the end of the queue. You'll need a bit of patience to make these yourself, but this recipe is well worth the effort. If you prefer glazed doughnuts, whisk 100 g (3½ oz) icing (confectioners') sugar, 4 Tbsp maple syrup and 1 Tbsp milk until smooth and use this mixture to glaze the cooled doughnuts.

Pour the apple cider into a saucepan. Bring to the boil, then reduce the heat and simmer over medium heat until reduced to 150 ml (5 fl oz). Leave to cool to lukewarm.

Combine the flours, yeast, salt and spices thoroughly in a large mixing bowl.

Whisk the sugar with the cider, egg yolks, oil and vanilla extract and add to the dry ingredients. Combine everything well. Dot with the butter and knead the dough for 5–10 minutes. Cover and leave to rise at room temperature for 2 hours.

Punch the dough down gently and roll it out on a lightly floured benchtop to just under 2 cm (¾ inch) thick. Cut twelve 7.5 cm (3 inch) circles, then cut a 2.5 cm (1 inch) hole from the centre of each circle. Transfer to a baking tray lined with baking paper and leave to rise for about 45 minutes.

Add enough oil to a heavy-based saucepan to come up about 5 cm (2 inches). Heat the oil to 180°C (350°F). Deep-fry the doughnuts and doughnut holes in batches, for about 30–60 seconds per side. Remove and drain on a thick layer of paper towel. Check the oil temperature every now and then.

Toss the doughnuts in cinnamon sugar after baking.

INGREDIENTS

*Makes 12 doughnuts and
12 doughnut holes*

500 ml (17 fl oz) apple cider
250 g (9 oz) plain flour
50 g (1¾ oz) wholemeal
plain flour
2 tsp dried yeast
½ tsp salt
1½ tsp ground cinnamon
¼ tsp allspice
¼ tsp ground cardamom
¼ tsp freshly grated nutmeg
55 g (2 oz) brown sugar
2 egg yolks
1 Tbsp oil
1 tsp vanilla extract
1 Tbsp butter, softened

Also:
Flour for dusting
Oil for deep-frying
Cinnamon and sugar

CHALLAH BUNS

Challah yeast pastries were first introduced to the Big Apple by Jewish migrants and have become an essential part of New York food. Filled with raisins and diced apples, challah is particularly tasty. Like all yeast pastry, challah buns are best eaten fresh, but if you have any leftovers, they are perfect for a bread pudding (see page 107).

INGREDIENTS

Makes 10

2 tsp dried yeast
1 Tbsp sugar
160 ml (5¼ fl oz) lukewarm water
60 ml (2 fl oz) mild olive oil
2 eggs
1 egg yolk
80 g (2¾ oz) honey
1 Tbsp salt
About 550 g (1¼ lb) plain flour

For the filling:
1 vanilla bean
80 g (2¾ oz) raisins
10 sprigs thyme
1 apple, very finely diced

Also:
Flour for dusting
1 egg yolk for glazing

Whisk the yeast and sugar into the warm water in a bowl and set aside for 10 minutes. Stir in the oil. Whisk in the eggs and egg yolk, one after the other. Add the honey and salt. Gradually add the flour and knead everything for about 5 minutes to make a pliable dough. Cover and leave to rise for about 1½ hours.

For the filling, halve the vanilla bean lengthwise and scrape the seeds into a saucepan. Add the vanilla bean, raisins, thyme and 240 ml (8 fl oz) water. Bring to the boil, then simmer until the liquid has evaporated. Remove from the heat, add the diced apple and set aside to cool. Discard the vanilla bean and thyme sprigs.

Divide the filling into 10 portions. Transfer the dough onto a floured benchtop and divide it into 10 portions. Roll each dough portion out to a 15 x 6 cm (6 x 2½ inch) rectangle.

Spread one portion of filling over the dough and roll up tightly from the long side. Keep rolling until the dough is about 35 cm (14 inches) long. Halve the roll across, then halve each of the resulting pieces lengthwise. Weave the four strands into a tight hashtag pattern so that they each run over and under an adjacent strand. Take each strand that is sitting underneath another and fold it back over the strand above it. Repeat and then tuck the ends under to make a knot. Transfer to a baking tray lined with baking paper. Repeat with the remaining dough and filling.

Brush the buns with egg yolk and leave to rise for 45 minutes.

Preheat the oven to 180°C (350°F) and bake the buns until golden brown, about 20 minutes.

NEW YORK
Christmas

Rose Ausländer
(Trans. Christopher Newton)

In dreamt up towers
bells peal off miracles

Stores are running temperatures
revolving doors swivel carols
into the clamour

Pines beam
electronic love

Yule-tide white dove
which realm
welcomed your news
in which pine
does your plumage
thicken

Today the lost kings
come to New York
with enchanted gifts
on a Harlem pilgrimage
to the Spirituals
pledge brotherhood at the dock
with the crew of a scuttled ship
propose in a bar
to their latest brandy-flames

In imagined towers
bells peal off miracles

★

INDEX OF RECIPES

LISA NIESCHLAG
★

LARS WENTRUP
★

JULIA CAWLEY
★

THE TEAM

Designer and photographer Lisa Nieschlag, who has family roots in New York, loves spending her time in the kitchen, cooking, baking, styling and photographing delicious food. Lars Wentrup is a designer and illustrator. Watching each page of a book being filled with text, images – life – has never lost its magic for Lars. Lisa and Lars have run an agency for communication design in the heart of Munster since 2001. A perfect team!

The internationally renowned photographer Julia Cawley recently returned to Germany, having lived in New York for five years. She lives and works in Hamburg, Germany's gateway to the world.

Julia and Lisa have set themselves a culinary challenge by publishing the popular food blog 'Liz & Jewels' together, where they present delicious recipes beautifully, each in her own, unique way. They are well-known for organising international food styling and photography workshops.

www.lizandjewels.com

THANKS

A big thank you to Julia, who immediately got herself onto a flight to New York as soon as the idea for this book was hatched and spared no effort to capture the Christmas mood in the Big Apple so beautifully in her photos.

We also would like to thank Agnes for her culinary support and Melissa for being on set and helping us bake – this book would never have been finished in time without you! Many thanks. We would also like to thank Friederike for her dedication and support.

Thanks to Tina for your incredible talent in organising, styling and baking, and thanks to Nik for your ideas and assistance in creating the illustrations.

Our special thanks go to Wolfgang Hölker, Dagmar Becker-Göthel and Franziska Grünewald for their confidence in us expanding the 'New York Christmas' series.

A big thank you also to our cooperation partners:
Botz, Geliebtes Zuhause, House Doctor and Davert

IMPRINT

Published in 2019 by Murdoch Books,
an imprint of Allen & Unwin
First published by Hölker Verlag in 2017

Murdoch Books Australia
83 Alexander Street
Crows Nest NSW 2065
Phone: +61 (0)2 8425 0100
murdochbooks.com.au
info@murdochbooks.com.au

Murdoch Books UK
Ormond House
26–27 Boswell Street
London WC1N 3JZ
Phone: +44 (0) 20 8785 5995
murdochbooks.co.uk
info@murdochbooks.co.uk

For corporate orders & custom publishing,
contact our business development team at
salesenquiries@murdochbooks.com.au.

DESIGN AND TYPESETTING:
Nieschlag + Wentrup, Büro für Gestaltung
www.nieschlag-und-wentrup.de

PHOTOS:
Lisa Nieschlag: Pages 2, 3, 12, 13, 14, 16, 17, 18, 19,
22, 23, 24, 27, 30, 32, 33, 36, 38, 39, 40, 45, 46, 48, 49,
52, 53, 54, 55, 56, 61, 62, 63, 64, 65, 67, 68, 69, 70, 71,
74, 77, 78, 79, 80, 81, 82, 86, 87, 88, 89, 90, 91, 93, 96,
97, 98, 99, 100, 105, 106, 108, 109, 110, 115, 116, 119
(www.lisanieschlag.de)
Julia Cawley: Pages 1, 7, 8, 9, 10, 20, 21, 28, 29, 34, 35,
42, 43, 50, 51, 58, 59, 72, 73, 84, 85, 94, 95, 102, 103,
112, 113, 120, 121, 122, 123, 124, 125
(www.juliacawley.com)
Anna Haas (portraits of Lisa Nieschlag and Lars
Wentrup): Page 126 (www.anna-haas.de)
Franziska Krauss (portraits of Julia Cawley): Pages 7
and 126

ILLUSTRATIONS: Lars Wentrup
RECIPE DEVELOPMENT: Agnes Prus
SET ASSISTANT: Melissa Lange
PRE-PRESS: FSM Premedia, Münster,
Birgit Depebrock
EDITOR: Franziska Grünewald

PUBLISHER: Corinne Roberts
TRANSLATORS: Claudia McQuillan-Koch; except p.121,
translated by Christopher Newton
ENGLISH-LANGUAGE EDITORS: Justine Harding and
Justin Wolfers
PRODUCTION DIRECTOR: Lou Playfair

TEXT CREDITS:
Page 10–11: Excerpt(s) from A CHRISTMAS MEMORY
by Truman Capote, copyright © 1956 and renewed
1984 by Truman Capote. Used by permission of
Random House, an imprint and division of Penguin
Random House LLC. All rights reserved.
Page 121: Rose Ausländer, New Yorker Weihnachten.
In: id., Hügel aus Äther unwiderruflich. Gedichte und
Prosa 1966-1975. © S. Fischer Verlag GmbH, Frankfurt
am Main 1984

© 2017 Hölker Verlag, in Coppenrath Verlag GmbH &
Co. KG Hafenweg 30, 48155 Münster, Germany

ISBN 9 781 76052 389 3 Australia
ISBN 9 781 76063 468 1 UK

 A cataloguing-in-publication entry is
available from the catalogue of the National
Library of Australia at nla.gov.au.

A catalogue record for this book is available from the
British Library.

Printed in China by C&C Offset Printing Co. Ltd.

OVEN GUIDE: You may find cooking times vary
depending on the oven you are using. For fan-forced
ovens, as a general rule, set the oven temperature to
20°C (70°F) lower than indicated in the recipe.

MEASURES GUIDE: We have used 20 ml (4
teaspoon) tablespoon measures. If you are using a 15
ml (3 teaspoon) tablespoon add an extra teaspoon of
the ingredient for each tablespoon specified.

MIX
Paper from
responsible sources
FSC® C008047

The paper in this book is FSC® certified.
FSC® promotes environmentally responsible,
socially beneficial and economically viable
management of the world's forests.